A Prayer for all Seasons

Written & Illustrated
By
Annette Tritico

Published by Franklin Publishers

Printed in the United States of America

For permissions, inquiries, or additional copies, contact:

Franklin Publishers

www.franklinpublishers.com

Acknowledgement

A special thanks to my sister, **Marietta Tritico Haym**, *for proofreading and assisting with the editing of this book.*

Dedication

To my parents, Joe and Anita Tritico;

For their unwavering love, selflessness, and the deep faith they planted in me from the very beginning. You were the epitome of Christian values, loyalty, honesty, and hard work—living examples of what it means to serve others. The countless ways you helped, loved, and mentored others will forever be etched in the hearts of so many. Your legacies continue to shine brightly in our community, and I am forever grateful to call you my parents.

Not only were you incredible parents to me, but you were also loving grandparents to your grandchildren. Your home was a sanctuary for your many friends, and you mentored hundreds of youth, leaving a lasting impact that will never be forgotten.

You were always there, offering a hand during times of crisis, celebrating life's joys, and making everyone around you feel special. Through your leadership, undying faith, compassion, and boundless love, you taught me the power of giving and the strength of community.

It is with deep gratitude and love that I dedicate this prayer book to you both as a small token of thanks for the countless blessings you have bestowed upon me and the world.

Preface

In the aftermath of Hurricane Rita in 2005, our community was devastated. Homes were lost, lives were uprooted, and the damage was overwhelming. As a registered nurse in the Lake Area community, I witnessed firsthand the physical pain and, perhaps even more profoundly, the psychological distress that so many of us were enduring. Working in the home health field, I was out in the community, visiting patients and their families, coordinating their care, and witnessing the deep sorrow on every face I encountered.

Everyone I met seemed to carry some kind of pain in their hearts, and they all needed encouragement, a word of hope. It was during this time that God placed it on my heart to write a prayer—my first prayer, in November of 2005—on the subject of gratitude. In the midst of devastation, I wanted to remind those around me of the importance of being grateful for what we had rather than focusing on what we had lost.

The response was overwhelming. The recipients of the prayers expressed deep gratitude for receiving them, saying they needed prayer more than ever during this difficult time. The next time I saw them, many asked for more prayers and wondered if I had a new one for December. And so, from that point on, I began writing prayers each month, inspired by the needs of my community.

For many years after that, each prayer was written through me by the Holy Spirit, guiding me to offer comfort, encouragement, and hope to the people of our community. These prayers were meant to help heal hearts and remind people that, despite the struggles, God was with them. I wrote to offer hope, peace, and faith—faith that God is always taking care of us and that, in His time, all will be well.

As you read through these prayers, I hope you find peace in your own journey. Whether you choose to reflect on a prayer from a specific month or find comfort in one that speaks to your heart, I pray that these words will bring healing and peace. May God bless you in all the seasons of your life.

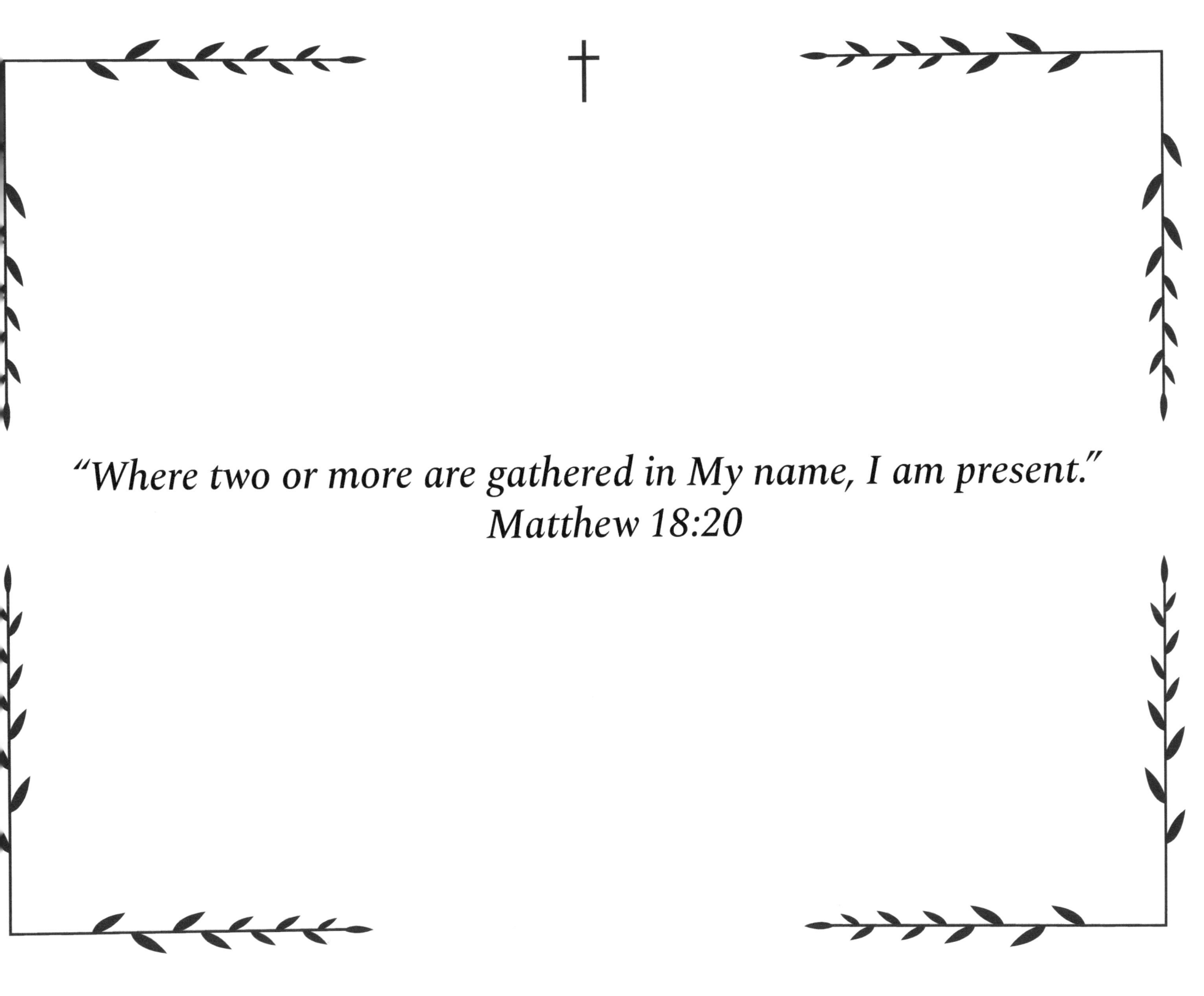

"Where two or more are gathered in My name, I am present."
Matthew 18:20

Table of Contents

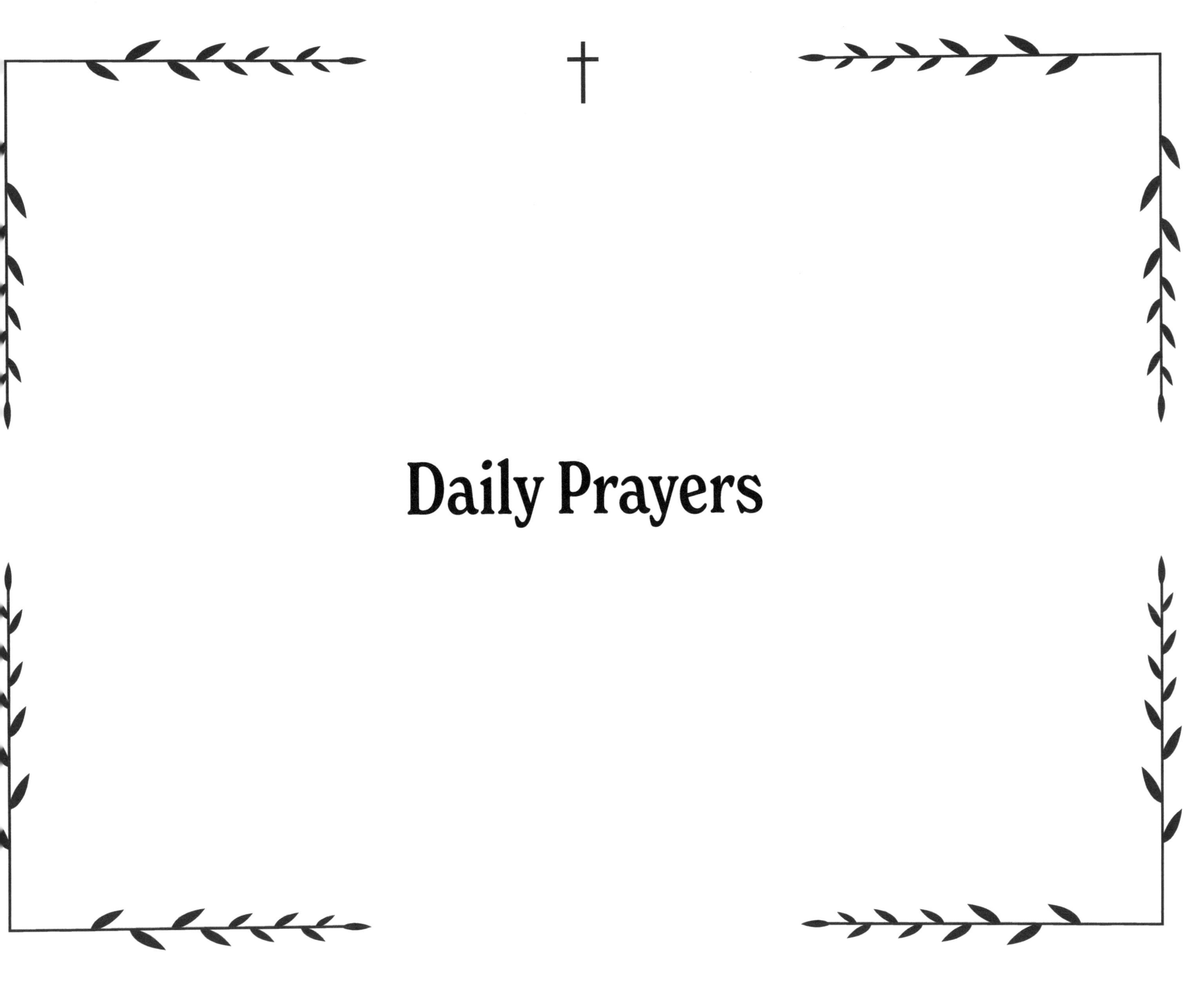

Daily Prayers

Good Morning

Dear Lord in Heaven,
Help me to make the best of this day.
To focus on the gifts you have given me, not what I do not have...
To walk with gratitude in my heart, not resentment,
To share love with others, not criticism,
To see the good in situations, not the bad,
To live in today, not yesterday or tomorrow,
To realize that it is not the cross we have to carry
But how we carry the cross that really matters.
Thank you for today, for it is the beginning of my future.
Help me to make the best of every minute.
I commit to live one day at a time and to:
LOVE, SERVE, AND LIVE life to its fullest!
In Jesus' name, I pray.
Amen

Help Me to Remember

Dear Lord, help me to remember to treat people the way I would like to be treated.
To respect others' opinions even though
They may be different from mine.
Help me Lord to not gossip
Or talk bad about others,
To think about what they may be going through
Before I say anything.
Help me to remember to pray for them,
Instead of criticizing them.
To see the positive in all situations instead of the negative,
To be patient and go the extra mile in all areas of my life,
To slow down and pay attention to the messages you send me
And realize it is only through You and You alone
That I will have true PEACE, SERENITY, AND SECURITY.
In Jesus' name, I pray,
Amen

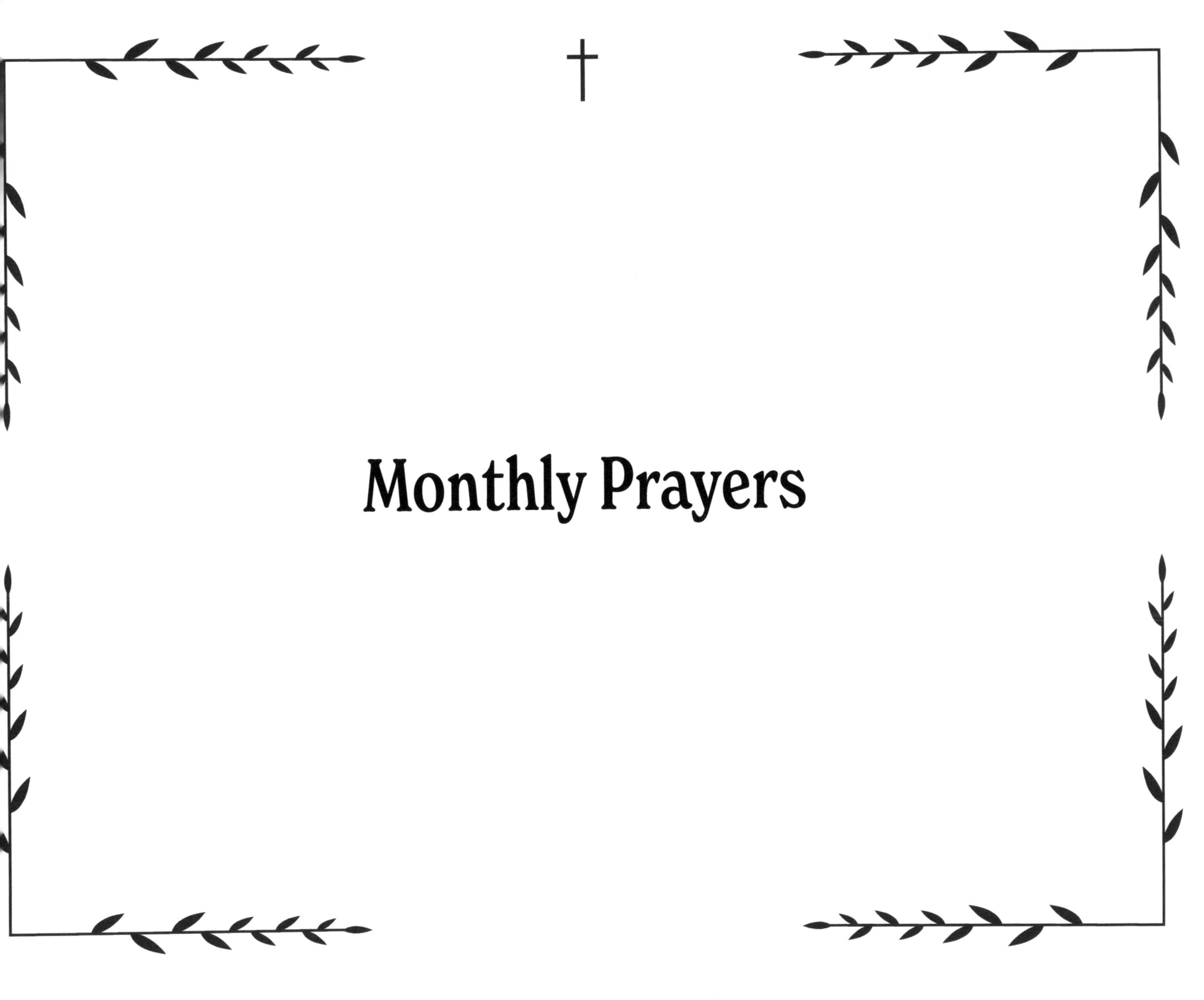

Monthly Prayers

January
New Year Meditation

I pray that I place the things I can't control in God's hands,
To ask for guidance in making important decisions or choices,
To set goals that will enhance my life,
And to accept that I am right where I need to be.
To learn from my mistakes, so I do not continue to repeat them.
And to take care of myself physically and mentally.
At the end of the day, to count my blessings, big or small,
And most of all, thank God for giving me another day
To live in this new year to come.
In Jesus' name, I pray,
Amen

February
Prayer to Love

Lord, help me to be an example of your love
By loving others unconditionally.
Help me to give those I love what they need most,
Whether it is attention, space, acceptance, or guidance.
Help me to know the difference between my needs and theirs.
Assist me, Lord, to love in an unselfish way
When I am alone, Lord, surround me with your love.
Please fill my heart with your faith from above,
So I can care for myself and for those I love.
In Jesus' Name, I pray.
Amen

March
Thank God for the Springtime

Thank you, God, for the beautiful days you created.
Help me to take the time to admire the beautiful blue sky,
Smell the perfume-scented flowers,
Walk in the cool green grass, to listen to the birds singing,
And to notice the new growth in my life.
Lord, help me to stay in today and not worry about tomorrow,
To trust that you have my life under control,
So I can appreciate the gifts you have given me and
Enjoy the springtime days,
one moment at a time, one day at a time.
In Jesus' name, I pray.
Amen

April
Easter Season

Help me, Lord, to remember the real meaning of Easter.
Help me to make sacrifices to help someone in need,
To take time to do kind deeds for someone
Who may be less fortunate.
To be slow to anger, less self-righteous
Or judgemental toward others.
Help me to stop and pray
About the choices I make or things I say.
To think in a positive way
And invite peace into my life today.
Help me to take time
To appreciate the life you gave me.
Thank you, Lord, for the gift of forgiveness
You gave us this special Easter season.
And, most of all, help me to remember what you did for all
Mankind... from now until eternity.
In Jesus' name, I pray,
Amen

May
The Gift of Rain

Help me to take the time to notice the blessings in my life,
To take time to see the rainbows in the sky and the flowers
That bloom from the rain sent from above.
Lord, help me to know that the rain in my life is...
Your way to help me grow.
Lord, please remind me that life is very simple.
And all I have to do is "Let go and let God,"
Pray and give my problems to You, then trust
You will take care of them.
When in doubt, help me to turn it over to You.
Thank you, Lord, for being there for me
when I did not know what to do.
For now I know you will carry me through.
In Jesus' name, I pray.
Amen

June
Thank God for the Summer Time

During the summer season, help us to
Enjoy the warm beautiful weather,
Take time to rest, relax, and enjoy life,
Appreciate the gifts you have given us
By spending quality time with our family and friends.
Help us to grow like a seed in our faith,
Blossom with hope for our future,
Share a smile and a hug with those we come in contact with
And focus on the gifts God has given us,
Instead of the trials and tribulations in our lives.
Trust that you will protect and take care of us,
No matter what we may be going through.
Help us to continue to grow, live and love life,
And to thank You for this wonderful summertime season.
In Jesus' name, we pray,
Amen

July
Freedom Prayer

Dear Lord, thank you for our freedom
To choose, to pray and to speak your word.
Help me, Lord, to make choices that are right and just,
To stand up for what I know is right.
To not be afraid to speak up for what you have taught me.
To choose the path of faith when troubled or in doubt.
To appreciate and pray for those who fight for our freedom.
Please guide the hands of our government
To make the decisions based on your law, not just man's desire.
Please protect us from any harm
As we journey through this world
And surround us with your love and protection,
So one day we may rejoice and live with you
And our loved ones in eternity forever.
In Jesus' name, I pray,
Amen

August
God's Attitude

What would you tell God about your attitude today?

Is it loving, patient and kind?

Is it caring and understanding toward others?

Is it unselfish and giving toward the people you are with?

Are you non-judgemental toward those who are different than you?

Are you exhibiting a positive attitude?

Is your outlook humble, merciful and grateful?

Heavenly Father, help me to stop and think about what I am saying.

Lord, help me to have the discipline to control my thoughts and behavior.

Please inspire me to be more like You.

Please give me a godlike attitude that is contagious,

To share your smile, thoughtfulness, and love with others.

Today, tomorrow and forever more.

In Jesus' name, we pray,

Amen

September
Gratitude Prayer

Dear Lord, please help me to be grateful
For the blessings in my life,
And to appreciate the things I may have taken for granted.
Thank you, Lord, for the tough times that you have taught me.
Help me to be strong, to practice being patient,
And to appreciate the good times.
Help me to forgive others, to forgive myself
And to accept when others forgive me.
To let go of resentments by loving others unconditionally.
Thank you, Lord, for my family, friends and co-workers.
Please help me to focus more on their needs or concerns,
And not as much as mine.
Lord, guide my thoughts and words to be of faith, kindness,
love, and peace during this season in life.
In Jesus' name, I pray,
Amen

October
Harvest Prayer

Thank you, Lord, for the Fall Season
That is filled with beautiful blue sky days
And fall-colored leaves blowing in the wind.
Help me to take the time to notice
The changes in the season,
To slow down, love life,
And make the best of the moment.
To accept the changes without having to
Always know the reason,
To realize You are the great and most powerful
With a plan designed just for me.
I trust You will not abandon or lead me astray,
Because I know You want the best for me everyday.
In Jesus' name, I pray,
Amen

November
Thanksgiving Prayer

Thank you, Lord, for the gifts you have given me.
Help me to be grateful for the blessings in my life.
Thank you for my family, my loved ones, and my friends.
Help me to show them unconditional love and acceptance.
Thank you for the sacrifices you made
For me to have salvation and eternal life.
Please help me to appreciate the good times and the bad,
For I know there is a reason for all.
Help me to know you will take care of me,
And that my prayers will be answered in your time and plans.
Thank you for comforting me
When I am afraid, anxious, or confused.
Help me, Lord, to trust, surrender, believe,
And receive your love and guidance,
No matter what is happening in my life.
In Jesus' name, I pray,
Amen

28

† December
Christmas Prayer

Dear Lord in heaven,
Help me to remember that Jesus is the real reason
For this holy season.
Help me to remember to give to those in need,
To share a smile with those who are near,
To share a positive word with those who may live in fear.
To remember, no matter what I may be going through,
You are taking care of it all.
Help me to be peaceful and joyful during this time of year,
To slow down amidst all the hustle and bustle,
And share a little laughter and cheer.
And when I think of a loved one who is not with me this year,
Help me to remember to say a special prayer
And know they are near.
God bless us and protect us during this holiday.
And most of all, help me to remember the real reason for the season.
In Jesus' name, I pray,
Amen

Prayers for God's Blessings

faith over fear

Prayers For God's Blessings

Lessons

Thank you, Lord, for the lessons you have taught me.

And may I realize they are blessings in disguise.

Help me to make choices that are good for me

And to have the courage to face difficult challenges.

Thank you, Lord, for the tough times,

For they teach me to appreciate life,

To learn the lessons you have put before me,

so I do not have to repeat them

And to know I am exactly where I need to be.

Help me to grow in my faith,

To know that you are always at my side.

Help me to trust in you and not be afraid,

Because I know you will carry me through it all.

In Jesus' name, I pray,

Amen

35

Prayers For God's Blessings

Loss and Grief

Dear Heavenly Father,

When I am experiencing a loss of some kind,

Help me to remember you are there

To fill my heart with your love.

That no mountain is too high to climb.

With you by my side, I will make it.

Help me to endure the adversities in my life.

And remind me the difficult times are blessings in disguise.

Give me the strength to cope with life's challenges

And to know all is your will.

Thank you, Lord, for the lessons you have taught me

And the courage to live my life with faith and hope.

For you are my savior and salvation.

In Jesus' name, I give you the glory!

In Jesus' name, I pray,

Amen

Pray

Prayers For God's Blessings

Live, Laugh, Love, and Pray

Dear Lord, help me to live my life to the fullest,

To make the best of the moment,

See the good and not the bad in my life situations,

Laugh at myself when I realize I am not perfect

Or when I make a mistake.

To know that you, too, have a sense of humor,

And that you want me to be happy,

To love like there is no tomorrow,

To tell those that I love how much I care,

To not fear love but to embrace love.

And, most of all, put my hands together and thank God.

For answering all of my prayers.

Because I trust that you know what is best for me.

In Jesus' name, I pray,

Amen

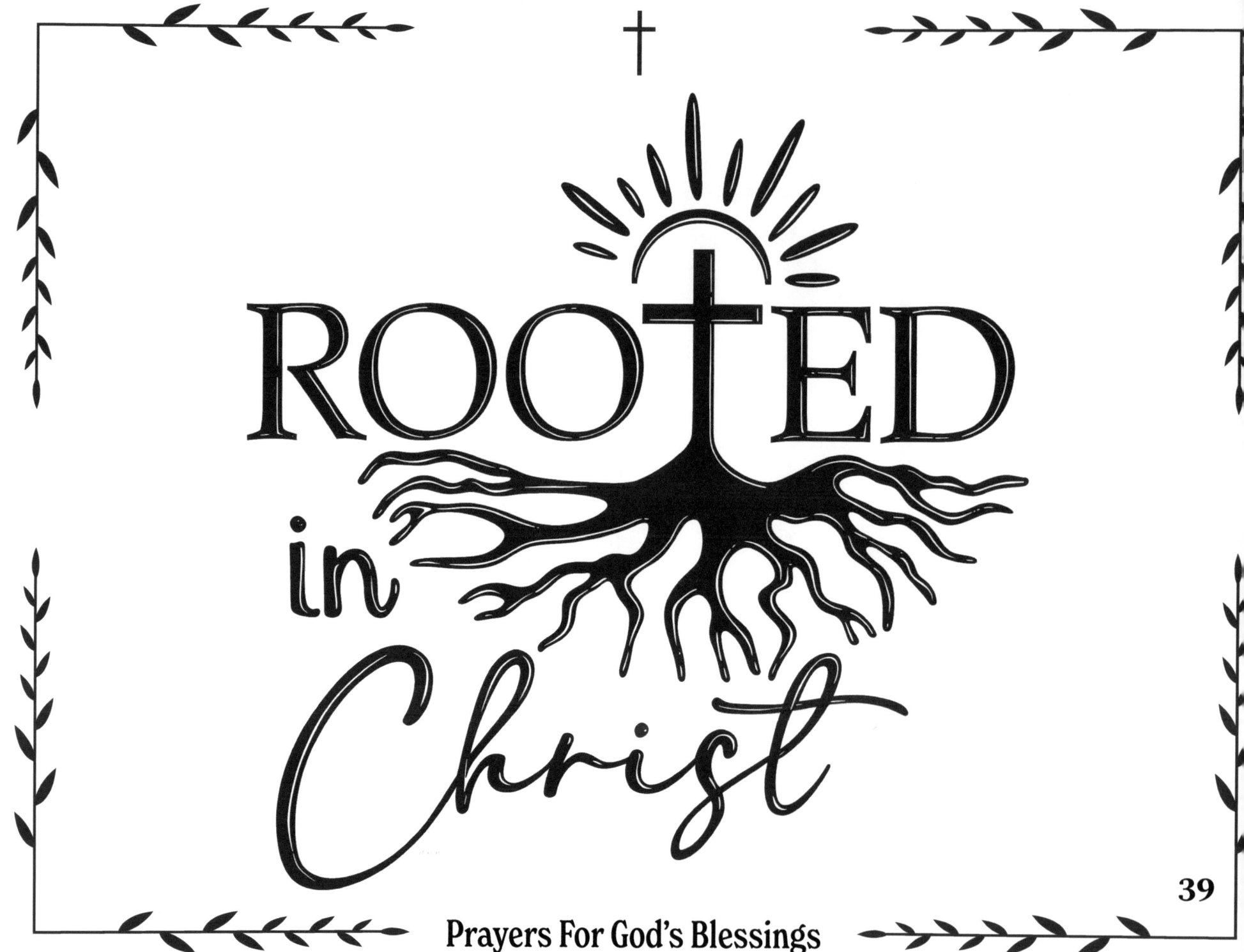

ROOTED in Christ

Prayers For God's Blessings

✝
Living Life

Dear Lord in heaven, help me to keep the promises I make,

To live my life in an honest way,

To mean what I say and to say what I mean.

Help me, Lord, to treat others the way I want to be treated

And to accept when things do not go my way.

Help me, Lord, to be authentic and real,

To treat others with respect and kindness,

To be loyal to my friends, coworkers, and loved ones.

To walk in my dignity and not allow anyone to take advantage of me,

To have healthy boundaries when I interact with others

And know that I have the ability to make healthy choices,

Even when I do not know what to do.

Please keep holding my hand, Lord, day by day,

So I will not be led astray.

Thank you, Lord, for blessing me with another day

To live the life you gave me.

In Jesus' name, I pray,

Amen

41

Prayers For God's Blessings

✝ Sacrifices

Thank you, Lord, for the sacrifices you made,
So that I would be forgiven for my sins.
Thank you for the life you have given me
And the lessons you have taught me,
So, that I will continue to learn from my past,
Live in today and look toward the future.
Thank you for the suffering you endured,
So I will have the insight to know my pain is only temporary
And to be grateful for everything in my life, whether good or bad.
Thank you, Lord, for the gift of eternal life.
Your resurrection taught me to never give up
And to always have faith and hope.
Thank you for always being present
To listen and answer my prayers
In the quiet moment of my heart.
I thank you, Lord, for taking care of me
And giving me peace and happiness.
In Jesus' name, I pray,
Amen

FAITH . HOPE . LOVE

43

Prayers For God's Blessings

Faith, Hope, and Love

Lord, help me to LOVE others unconditionally
Without judging them,
To instill faith in those who are in doubt
By being an example of your love,
To give HOPE to those who are in pain
By sharing your word,
To remember that LOVE, HOPE, and FAITH are the keys
To peace and serenity.
In Jesus' name, I pray,
Amen

45

Letting Go of Control

I pray that I place the things I can not control in God's hands,

To ask for guidance in making important decisions or choices,

To set goals that will enhance my life

And accept I am right where I need to be.

May I show appreciation and gratitude to those I love and care about.

And may I be a positive example to others.

May I learn from my mistakes, so I do not repeat them,

And take care of myself physically and mentally.

And, most of all, at the end of the day,

Count my blessings that are big or small,

That I thank God for them all.

In Jesus' name, I pray,

Amen

47

Prayers For God's Blessings

A Prayer of Healing

May God bless and heal me this day.

May he carry me through whatever I am going through.

May God comfort me when I am in pain,

Strengthen me when I feel weak,

Hold my hand when I am alone,

Give me courage if I am afraid,

And give me the patience, wisdom, and insight

To recover as soon as possible.

May the grace of God surround me and heal me.

In Jesus' name, I pray,

Amen

"Trust, Surrender, Believe, Receive."